HERMIT CRABS

HERMIT CRABS

by Sylvia A. Johnson

Photographs by Kazunari Kawashima

A Lerner Natural Science Book

Lerner Publications Company • Minneapolis

Sylvia A. Johnson, Series Editor

Translation of original text by Wesley M. Jacobsen

The publisher wishes to thank Franklin H. Barnwell, Professor and Head of the Department of Ecology and Behavioral Biology, University of Minnesota, for his assistance in the preparation of this book.

Additional photographs by: p. 10, Atsushi Sakurai; p. 13, Jeff Rotman.

The glossary on page 46 gives definitions and pronunciations of words shown in **bold type** in the text.

LIBRARY OF CONGRESS CATALOGING-IN-PUBLICATION DATA

Johnson, Sylvia A.
   Hermit crabs / by Sylvia A. Johnson : photographs by Kazunari Kawashima.
     p.   cm.—(A Lerner natural science book)
   "Text adapted from Hermit crabs...by Kazunari Kawashima."—T.p. verso.
   Summary: Describes the physical characteristics, habits, and natural environment of the hermit crab.
Includes index.
ISBN: 0-8225-1488-5
   1. Hermit crabs—Juvenile literature. [1. Hermit crabs.] I. Kawashima, Kazunari, ill. II. Kawashima, Kazunari. Yadokari. III. Title. IV. Series
QL444.M33J65   1989
595.3'842—dc20   89-8221
                            CIP
                            AC

This edition first published 1989 by Lerner Publications Company.
Text copyright © 1989 by Lerner Publications Company.
Photographs copyright © 1988 by Kazunari Kawashima.
Text adapted from HERMIT CRABS copyright © 1988 by Kazunari Kawashima.
English translation rights arranged with Akane Shobo Company, Ltd., through Japan Foreign-Rights Centre

International Standard Book Number: 0-8225-1488-5
Library of Congress Catalog Number: 89-8221

1 2 3 4 5 6 7 8 9 10 98 97 96 95 94 93 92 91 90 89

Hermit crabs inside their snail-shell houses

Take a walk along any rocky ocean shore, and you will be sure to see some fascinating creatures. Many kinds of plants and animals make their homes on the rocks or in the shallow pools of water left behind by the tide.

The animals of the seashore are often strange in appearance and behavior. Some look more like plants than animals, with stem-like bodies and waving tentacles. Others spend their lives concealed inside shells or other hard coverings.

One of the most unusual seashore animals is the little hermit crab, which makes its home inside a snail shell. In the following pages, you will discover what kind of animal the hermit crab is and why it lives in a borrowed shell.

Opposite: This tide pool on an ocean shore provides a home for hermit crabs and many other kinds of animals.

THE SEASHORE COMMUNITY

Hermit crabs and other animals of the seashore live in a very different environment than the creatures of the ocean. The seashore world is one of constant change. On many ocean shores, the water level rises and falls twice each day. At **high tide**, the water creeps up on the land, covering the rocks and sand. When it is **low tide**, the water falls back, uncovering the shore and leaving behind only shallow **tide pools** among the rocks.

The animals of the seashore must be able to survive this twice-a-day change in their environment. Many of them must spend half of their lives submerged in water and half exposed to air and sun. Others have to avoid being swept away when the waves splash over them at high tide. Whether they are searching for food or hiding from enemies, the animals of the seashore must suit their behavior to the rhythms of the daily tides.

In most seashore communities, there are different life zones, or "neighborhoods," inhabited by different kinds of animals. Farthest up on the shore is the high intertidal zone, a region covered by water only when the tide is at its highest. This zone is home to some of the strange shell-covered animals known as barnacles. Shore crabs are also common here.

Animals living on this rocky seashore include (1) crustaceans called barnacles, which attach themselves to the rocks; (2) shore sponges; (3) chitons, mollusks with flat, segmented shells.

The middle intertidal zone is covered and uncovered by the tide twice each day. In this region of tidal pools lives a wide variety of creatures, including barnacles, mussels, sponges, and hermit crabs.

The low intertidal zone is almost always covered by water. Only the lowest tides expose this region. The many animals that live here—sea stars, sea anemones, tube worms, shrimp, and fish—have much in common with the animals of the ocean floor.

8

Barnacles live inside hard, shell-like coverings that are permanently attached to seashore rocks. They get food by filtering small animals and plants from the water with their feathery legs.

Other animals of the tide pools include quick-moving crabs *(above left)* and sea stars that creep over the rocks on tiny tube feet *(above center)*. Gorgonians *(above right)* and tube worms *(below left)* are animals that look like plants and that never move from one spot. Tide-pool swimmers include small fish brought in by the tide *(below center)* and the graceful nudibranch *(below right)*, a shell-less relative of the marine snail.

9

True crabs like the one shown above are common along many ocean shores. This crab is holding a dead fish in one of its powerful claws.

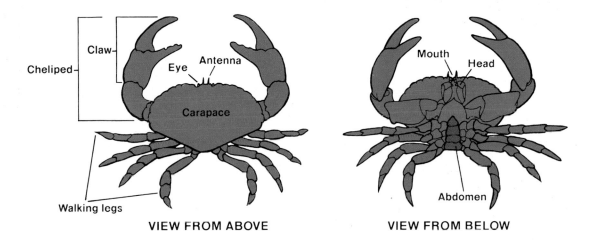

Claw

Cheliped

Eye Antenna

Carapace

Walking legs

VIEW FROM ABOVE

Mouth Head

Abdomen

VIEW FROM BELOW

These drawings show the parts of a true crab's body. Hermit crabs belong to another group of crabs and have slightly different body parts.

Many kinds of crabs are members of the seashore community. These **crustaceans** can often be seen scurrying over the rocks or walking on the bottoms of tide pools.

Like their relatives the lobsters and shrimps, most crabs have a hard outer covering over their soft bodies. They also have many jointed limbs, or **appendages**, which are used for different purposes. Some appendages tear up a crab's food, while others are used for walking.

A crab's most important appendages are its two large **chelipeds**, which have powerful claws at their ends. These claws are used to hold onto objects, to defend the crab against enemies, and for many other purposes.

11

LIFE INSIDE A BORROWED SHELL

Hermit crabs have many features in common with their relatives, but they are not considered **true crabs.** Instead, scientists place them in a special group known as **anomuran crabs.** Other members of this group are mole crabs and robber, or coconut, crabs.

There is one major difference between hermit crabs and true crabs like the one pictured on the previous page. A true crab has a short abdomen that is folded up under the large shell on its back. A hermit crab, on the other hand, has a long abdomen that sticks out at the rear end of its body. Because its abdomen does not have a hard covering, the hermit crab must use a borrowed shell to protect this part of its body.

The empty shells of marine snails are the ones most often used by hermit crabs. Marine snails, like land snails, are **univalve mollusks,** animals whose soft bodies are concealed inside spiral shells. Whelks and periwinkles are two common kinds of marine snails found on many seashores.

When marine snails die, their bodies decay, but their hard shells remain on the sea bottom or on the shore. These empty shells make perfect homes for hermit crabs.

Left: A hermit crab with its body outside its snail shell. The shell has been cut in half so that you can see the spiral inside. *Above:* When the crab goes inside the shell, its body fits around the spiral's curves.

The bodies of hermit crabs are specially suited to fit inside snail shells. Most marine snails have shells with spirals that turn to the right. The abdomens of most hermit crabs are also curved to the right, as you can see in the photograph on the opposite page.

A hermit crab's appendages are well suited to life inside a borrowed shell. Compared to true crabs, hermit crabs have fewer appendages on their abdomens, particularly on the right side. This makes it easier for a crab to fit into the right-turning spiral of a snail shell. The appendages on the end of a hermit's abdomen are specially designed to get a good grip on the shell and hold it in place as the crab moves along. The photograph and drawing on the opposite page show how this is done.

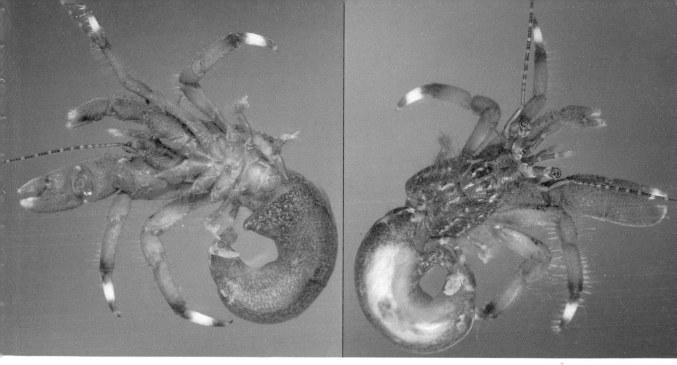

A hermit crab viewed from below (left) and above (right). Looking at the crab from below, you can see the small legs on the middle of the body that help to hold the animal inside a snail shell. The view from above shows how the crab's long, unprotected abdomen curves to the right.

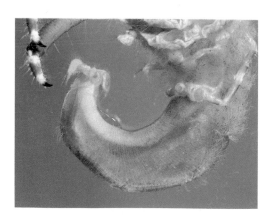

At the tip of a hermit crab's abdomen are small appendages used to grip the shell's spiral.

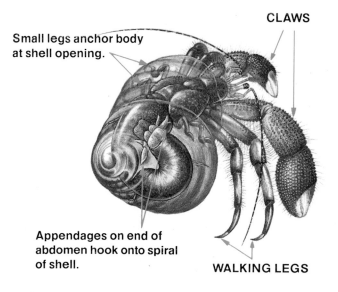

CLAWS

Small legs anchor body at shell opening.

Appendages on end of abdomen hook onto spiral of shell.

WALKING LEGS

 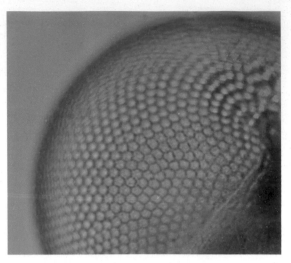

Left: A hermit crab's antennules (green arrow) and antennae (red arrow) are important sense organs. *Right:* This photograph shows the many tiny lenses in a crab's compound eye.

Although hermit crabs have appendages and abdomens that are different from other kinds of crabs, some of their body parts are very similar. Like all their relatives, hermit crabs have **compound eyes** consisting of many tiny lenses. The images that crabs see with these eyes are also made up of many pieces, like a mosaic picture.

The eyes of crabs are located at the ends of moveable **eyestalks**. When a hermit crab withdraws into its shell, its eyestalks bend forward so that they don't catch on the edge of the shell.

Like other crabs, hermit crabs have special sense organs on their heads that they use to pick up information about their environment. A pair of **antennules**, located between a crab's eyes, are sensitive to odors and are used to locate food. On the outside of the eyes are two long **antennae**, with

which the crab touches objects around it. In the photograph above, two hermit crabs are using their antennae to get acquainted.

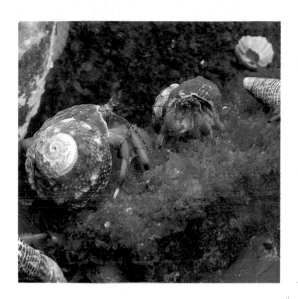

IN SEARCH OF A GOOD MEAL

Hermit crabs that live along the seashore do not have a great many choices when it comes to food. Luckily, most of them are not fussy eaters.

Some hermit crabs eat the seaweed that grows in the water and on the rocks along the shore (left). One of the favorite foods of these crabs is a green seaweed called **sea lettuce,** which grows in flat sheets or ribbons on the seashore rocks. In the photograph above, several hermit crabs can be seen grazing on a patch of sea lettuce.

This crab's long antennae have feathery tips that are used to catch tiny animals floating in the water. The animals serve as part of the crab's food supply.

In addition to feeding on plants, many hermit crabs eat animals. And they don't mind at all if the animals happen to be dead. In fact, these crabs are sometimes called janitors of the tide pools because they get rid of the bodies of dead fish and other creatures.

A hermit crab uses its sensitive antennules to pick up the odor of a dead animal in the water. When the crab locates a possible meal, it hurries to the spot, guided by the smell. Sometimes, many hermit crabs will gather around the body of a dead fish. In a very short time, they consume the flesh, leaving only the bones behind. In this way, the little crustaceans help to keep the seashore clean.

This hermit crab is about to make a meal of a dead goby fish.

THE DEVELOPMENT OF HERMIT CRABS

When it is time for hermit crabs to mate and have young, they behave much like other kinds of crabs. A male hermit usually finds a partner by means of odors that female crabs send out when they are ready to mate.

After a male locates a female of his species, he may spend some time with her before mating. Some male hermit crabs use their claws to stroke and tap their partners' claws. In some species, a male will take hold of the female's snail shell with his claws and carry her around for a while before they mate.

In order to mate, hermit crabs have to climb out of their shell houses. In the act of mating, the male's sperm cells enter the female's body. Here they unite with the female's egg cells, and new life begins to grow inside the eggs.

Hermit crab eggs go through their development within the safety of the female crab's shell. The female lays her eggs inside the shell, where they become attached to appendages on her abdomen. She will carry the eggs around with her until they are ready to hatch.

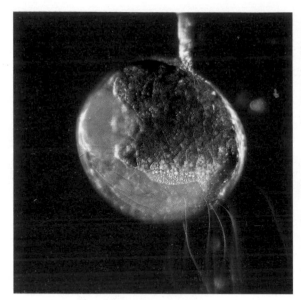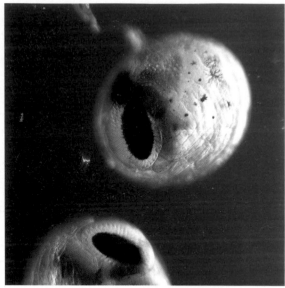

These greatly enlarged photographs show two stages in the development of hermit crab eggs. In the picture on the left, the body of the little crab has begun to grow inside the jelly-covered egg. At a later stage of growth, a single large black eye can be seen inside each egg (right).

Like the eggs of all crustaceans, hermit crabs eggs are covered with a jelly-like material. At first, the tiny eggs are transparent. As the baby hermit crabs inside the eggs grow, their bodies can be seen through the jelly covering. The large black eyes of the developing crabs are particularly noticeable.

After finishing their development inside the female crab's shell, the eggs are ready to hatch. By this time, they are dark in color, their jelly coverings filled by the bodies of the little crabs.

Although many adult hermit crabs are creatures of the

24

The shell of this female hermit crab has been cut open so that you can see the dark-colored eggs inside. Most hermit crab females produce several hundred eggs at one time.

shore, baby hermit crabs cannot survive out of water. When her eggs are ready to hatch, a female hermit crab must release them into the ocean.

At high tide, the female lifts her body out of the shell and shakes her abdomen vigorously. The eggs attached to the appendages on her abdomen split open, and the little creatures inside fall into the water. (The photograph on the following pages shows female hermit crabs releasing their young in the water.)

Female hermit crabs releasing their eggs in the water

27

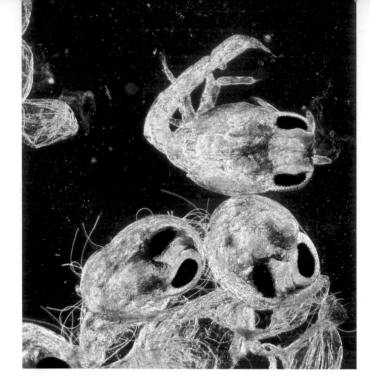

A zoea is the first stage in the development of a young hermit crab. The tiny creature is only about 2 millimeters (less than 1/8 inch) in length.

When it hatches, a baby hermit crab doesn't look much like an adult crab. Like insects, crabs and other crustaceans go through several stages of development before they become adults. During this period, they are known as **larvae** (singular, larva).

A hermit crab larva in the early stages of development is called a **zoea**. A zoea has large bulging eyes and a long, shrimp-like body. It has few of the appendages of an adult hermit crab. The zoea spends most of its time swimming in the ocean and feeding on other tiny animals. Sometimes the developing crab becomes a meal for larger sea creatures like fish.

A hermit crab zoea grows rapidly by means of **molting**. When the larva molts, it sheds the hard outer covering of its

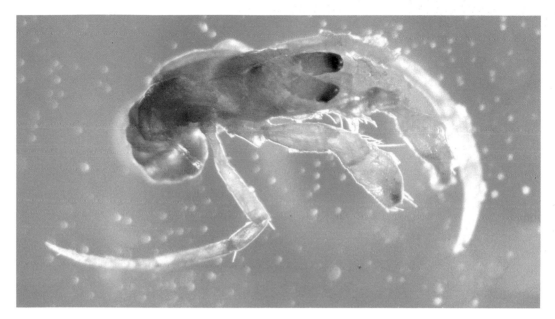

When it becomes a glaucothoë, a young hermit crab looks much more like an adult. After one more molt, its development will be complete.

body. Underneath, a new, larger covering has already developed. The zoea usually molts three times on the bottom of the ocean, each time growing larger and adding more appendages.

After its third molt, the hermit crab enters a new stage of development. Now known as a **glaucothoë**, it looks much more like an adult hermit crab. After one more molt, the little animal will become an adult and take its place among the hermit crabs that live along the seashore. Even before it makes this final change, the glaucothoë may protect its abdomen by putting it inside a snail shell.

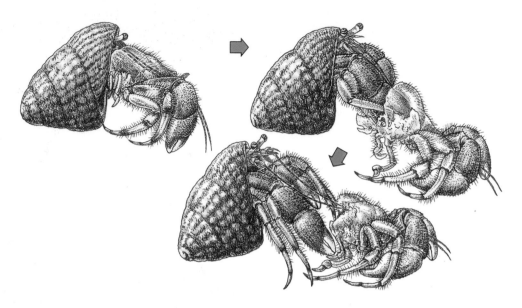

A hermit crab molting. During the time that it is shedding its old exoskeleton, the crabs keeps its soft abdomen inside the protective snail shell.

Both as a larva and an adult, a hermit crab grows by molting. Its **exoskeleton**, the hard outer covering of its body, does not expand as human skin does. Instead, it must be shed and replaced by a new, larger exoskeleton.

When a hermit crab molts, the exoskeleton on the back part of its body begins to split. Sticking its upper body out of the shell house, the crab works its way out of the old covering. First its eyestalks are uncovered, then its walking legs, and finally the large legs with the claws. Underneath, there is a new exoskeleton, which is soft at this stage of its development. The hermit crab retires into its snail shell until the new covering hardens.

This hermit crab has just finished molting. It is hiding inside its shell until its new body covering becomes hard. To the right of the crab is its old exoskeleton.

When a hermit crab is young, it molts frequently. After it becomes an adult, the crustacean molts only two or three times a year.

A hermit crab uses its claws to check out the size of a new snail shell.

LOOKING FOR A NEW HOME

A hermit crab produces a new and larger exoskeleton from time to time, but its shell house never gets any bigger. As the crab grows, it must replace the shell that protects its abdomen.

When its snail shell becomes a little snug, a hermit crab starts looking for a new home. If it finds an empty shell, the crab carefully checks it out. It uses its large claws to "measure" the size of the shell inside and out. If the snail shell seems to be a good size, the hermit crab cleans it out. It dumps out any sand inside and picks out pebbles with its claws.

When its new home is ready, the crab quickly pulls its abdomen out of the old shell and sticks it into the new one. Only after it is completely satisfied with its new house will the crab leave the old shell behind.

Sometimes a hermit crab has difficulty finding a new, larger shell. Many snail shells on the seashore are still occupied by snails. Others already have crabs living inside them. When a hermit crab can't locate a new shell, it may try to steal one from another hermit crab.

Above: The hermit crab moves into the new shell, carefully inserting its abdomen into the shell spiral. *Right:* Before it lets go of the old shell, the crab makes sure that the new one suits its needs.

The photographs on these two pages show one hermit crab stealing a shell from another hermit crab. *Left:* The attacker (top) holds onto the victim's shell with its claws and hits the shell with its own shell. *Right:* When the victim sticks its head out (left), the attacker grabs the crab and begins to pull it out of the shell.

When a hermit crab wants to take another crab's house, it uses a special method. First, it hits its own shell again and again against the shell it is trying to take. The noise bothers the shell's occupant so much that it pokes its head out. Then the attacker grabs the crab with its claws and drags it out of the shell. The house stealer quickly moves into the empty shell, leaving its former owner out in the open.

The crab that loses its house usually has no choice but to move into the shell left by the attacker. Sometimes the empty shell is too small. At other times, the victorious crab refuses to let go of its old shell. Then the loser is left without any protection. If the crab doesn't find a new house quickly, it may be in for a lot of trouble.

The attacker (right) moves into the shell abandoned by the other crab.

Above: A hermit crab withdraws into its shell to avoid a curious goby. *Left:* A shell provides no protection for a hermit crab attacked by a sea star.

PROTECTION FROM ENEMIES

A hermit crab without a shell house is open to attack by many enemies. With a shell to protect it, the crab can often defend itself. It can withdraw inside the shell, blocking the opening with its large claws.

Not all ocean **predators** are stopped by a hermit crab's protective shell. Some fish can bite through a snail shell. An octopus has hard, horny jaws that can crush a shell.

A sea star doesn't even have to destroy a hermit crab's shell to get to the crab. It uses the suction cups on the underside of its body to grip the shell. Then the sea star pushes its stomach out through its mouth opening, which is also located on its lower surface. With its stomach inside out, the predator digests the hermit crab while it is still inside the shell.

A hermit crab being eaten by a sea star. The predator has pulled the crab, shell and all, inside the mouth opening on the lower surface of its body. It will insert its stomach into the shell and digest the crab's body.

A hermit crab drops one of its claws (red arrow) to escape an attack by another hermit crab.

When a hermit crab withdraws into its shell, it has to move fast or a predator may grab it by a claw or a leg. If this happens, the hermit has another method of defending itself. It can break off an appendage at a special point called a **breaking plane**. The predator is left holding only the appendage, while the hermit crab quickly retreats into the safety of its shell.

Dropping off an appendage causes no serious injury to the crab. A layer of cells forms over the stump so that little blood is lost. What is even more amazing is that the crab can grow a new appendage to replace the missing one. At first, the new appendage is small, but it gradually becomes larger as the crab goes through several molts. Eventually, it is the same size as the appendage that was lost.

This ability to break off limbs and grow new ones is shared by all crabs and many other kinds of crustaceans.

Above: This hermit crab has a tiny claw (red arrow) that is gradually replacing one lost about 10 days earlier. *Right:* A claw dropped off by a hermit crab (right) is smooth and clean at the breaking plane. The other claw, which was torn off of a dead crab, has a ragged end.

Like some hermit crabs, clown fish have a special relationship with sea anemones. Because the fish are not affected by an anemone's poison, they can hide from predators within its deadly tentacles.

Some hermit crabs have a very special way of protecting themselves from predators. These crabs form partnerships with certain kinds of **sea anemones**, animals with stalk-like bodies topped by many tentacles. A partnership between a hermit crab and an anemone serves the needs of both creatures. Here is how it works.

Sea anemones usually attach themselves to rocks along the shore or in the ocean. If a hermit crab wants an anemone as a partner, it will poke and prod one with its claws until the anemone releases its hold on the rock. Then the crab picks up the anemone and puts the animal on top of its own shell house. The anemone uses the adhesive disk at the base of its body to attach itself to the shell. Here it will remain until the crab moves into a new shell.

How does a sea anemone provide protection for a hermit crab? Anemones carry a stinging poison in their tentacles.

This hermit crab is carrying several sea anemones on its shell.
The anemone on the right has its tentacles partially withdrawn.

41

1) A hermit crab accompanied by three anemones checks out a new shell.

Predators know about this poison and will often avoid a crab that is accompanied by an anemone. If a predator is foolish enough to attack the crab, it may be driven away by the anemone's poison sting.

The anemone also gains something from this strange partnership. Anemones normally stay in one place. But if an anemone travels with a hermit crab, it may have an opportunity to find more food. It may also be able to eat some of the scraps left over from the crab's meals.

Because this partnership is so important to both animals, it does not end when the hermit crab moves to a new shell. The anemone usually changes homes too. The photographs on these two pages show how the transfer is made.

2) The crab moves into its new house.

3) Using its claws and front legs, the crab detaches an anemone from the old shell.

4) Anemone Number Two is removed.

5) The crab puts the third anemone on its new shell.

6) Once on the new shell, the anemones move around until they find the most comfortable position. With its three partners in place, the hermit crab goes about its business.

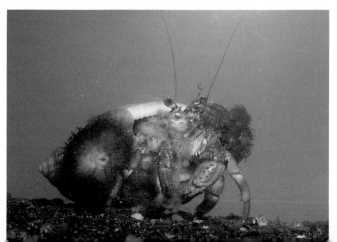

Pagurus lanuginosus

HERMIT CRABS
AROUND THE WORLD

Hermit crabs live on the shores of many of the world's oceans. Some of the most common hermits belong to a scientific genus, or group, called *Pagurus*.

Pagurus crabs can be found on the Atlantic and Pacific coasts of North America, as well as in many other parts of the world. Most of the crabs pictured in this book, including the three shown on this page, are members of this group.

One characteristic of almost all *Pagurus* crabs is the difference in the size of their two claws. The claw on the right side is always larger than the one on the left. (You can see this difference in the crabs shown here.) *Pagurus* crabs often use their right claws to block the entrances to their shell houses.

Pagurus japonicus

Pagurus dubius

Dardanus megistos

Dardanus guttatus

Although many hermit crabs make their homes on the seashore, others live in different environments. The two crabs shown above are found in the warm waters near coral reefs. Below is a hermit crab that spends all of its adult life on land. A member of the genus *Coenobita*, it lives on beaches above the high tide line and makes its house in snail shells that have been washed ashore.

Coenobita cavipes

GLOSSARY

anomuran (an-uh-MYUR-ehn) crabs—crustaceans that belong to the scientific group Anomura. These animals resemble true crabs in many ways, but their abdomens and some of their appendages are different.

antennae (an-TEN-ee)—sense organs on the heads of crabs and other crustaceans. Most hermit crabs have two long antennae, which are used to touch objects.

antennules (an-TEN-yuhls)—sense organs on the heads of crabs and other crustaceans. Most hermit crabs have two short antennules, which pick up odors.

appendages (uh-PEN-dij-uhs)—small body parts connected to the main sections of an animal's body. True crabs usually have 19 pairs of appendages, including their mouthparts and legs. Most hermit crabs have fewer appendages on their abdomens than true crabs.

breaking plane—a point on a crab's appendage where breakage can occur without injuring the crab

chelipeds (KEE-luh-peds)—legs that have claws, or chelae, at their ends

compound eyes—eyes made up of many tiny lenses, each of which sees a separate image.

crustaceans (krus-TAY-shuns)—animals such as crabs, lobsters, and shrimps that have segmented bodies covered with a hard protective material. Crustaceans belong to the scientific class Crustacea.

exoskeleton (ek-so-SKEL-ih-tun)—the hard covering of a crustacean's body, which provides protection and support to the soft body parts. The abdomens of hermit crabs do not have this covering.

eyestalks—the projections on a crab's head that bear the animal's eyes. Most crabs can bend or lower their eyestalks to protect their eyes.

glaucothoë (glau-KAHTH-ih-wee)—a hermit crab larva in its second, and final, stage of development

high tide—the highest point to which water regularly rises on the seashore. Many spots on the shore have two high tides during every 24-hour period. Tidal changes are caused by the pull of the sun's and the moon's gravity on the earth. Twice each month, high tide is higher than usual because the moon and the sun are positioned in such a way that they exert a combined pull on the earth.

larvae (LAR-vee)—young animals in an immature state of development. Many crustaceans, insects, fish, and amphibians such as frogs and toads go through a larval stage before they become adults.

low tide—the lowest point to which water regularly falls on the seashore. Many spots on the shore have two low tides during every 24-hour periods. Twice each month, there are unusually low tides caused by the position of the earth in relation to the moon and the sun.

molting—shedding an old exoskeleton to make way for a new one that has formed underneath

predators—animals that kill and eat other animals

sea anemones (uh-NEHM-ih-nees)—animals with soft tube-like bodies topped by many tentacles. The tentacles, which surround an anemone's mouth, contain cells that produce a stinging poison. Anemones are members of a scientific group callled Cnidaria, which also includes corals and jellyfish.

sea lettuce—a green seaweed that often grows in sheets or ribbons on seashore rocks. Like most seaweeds, it is a kind of alga, a simple plant without roots, leaves, or flowers.

tide pool—a pool of water left on a rocky seashore after the tide has receded

true crab—the most common kind of crab, with a short, folded abdomen and a body completely covered by an exoskeleton. Familiar shore crabs such as ghost and fiddler crabs belong to this group, which scientists call Brachyura.

univalve mollusk (YU-nih-valv MOL-usk)—an animal whose soft body is hidden inside a single spiral-shaped shell. Marine and land snails belong to this group of mollusks. Oysters and clams are bivalve mollusks, animals whose shells have two parts.

zoea (zo-EE-uh)—a crab larva in the first stage of its development

INDEX

abdomen, 12, 14, 16
anomuran crabs, 12
antennae, 16-17
antennules, 16, 20
appendages, 11, 14, 16, 23, 28; breaking off of, 38

barnacles, 7, 8
breaking plane, 38

chelipeds, 11
claws, 11, 23, 38, 44
coconut crab, 12
crabs: anomuran, 12; shore, 7, 11; true, 12, 14
crustaceans, 11, 24

eggs, 23; development of, 24-25; hatching of, 25
exoskeleton, 11, 30
eyes, compound, 16
eyestalks, 16

fish, 8, 36
food of hermit crabs, 19-20

glaucothoë, 29

high intertidal zone, 7
high tide, 7, 8

larvae of hermit crabs, 28-29
lobsters, 11
low intertidal zone, 8
low tide, 7, 8

mating, 23
middle intertidal zone, 8
mole crabs, 12

molting, 28-29, 30, 38
mussels, 8

North America, hermit crabs in, 44

octopus, 36

Pagurus, 44
periwinkles, 12
predators of hermit crabs, 36, 38; protection against, 38, 40, 42

reproduction, 23-25
robber crabs, 12

sea anemones, 8; partnerships of, with hermit crabs, 40, 42
sea lettuce, 19
seashore: animals of, 5, 7-8; environment of, 7-8, 19
sea stars, 8, 36
seaweed, 19
"shell stealing," 32, 34
shrimps, 8, 11
snails, marine, 12; shells of, used by hermit crabs, 14, 23, 29, 32, 34, 36

tide pools, 7, 8
tides, 7
tube worms, 8

univalve mollusks, 12

whelks, 12

zoea, 28-29